Skill: Identifying Who, What, When, Where, How, Why

Name _____

Silence Is Broken

Write an outline for a newspaper article based on the experience in this story. Use complete sentences.

Who: _____
_____

What: _____
_____

When: _____
_____

Where: _____
_____

How: _____
_____

Why: _____
_____

Write a headline for your article.
_____
_____

Extension: On a map of Canada, locate where Gary's story takes place. Use the clues provided in this story.

Skill: Organizing Data

Are You Superstitious?

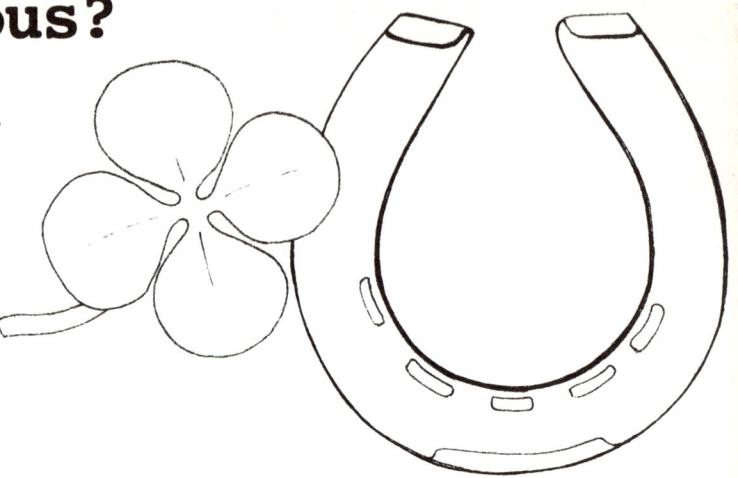

Are you superstitious? Most people, even those who claim not to be, act superstitiously at one time or another. Superstition is a belief that a certain action or event can cause or foretell another possibly unrelated event. Where does this belief come from?

Throughout history, superstitions have been found in every human society. Many superstitions date back to the earliest times. For example, if a black cat crosses your path, it is thought bad luck will follow. A recent superstition claims that if one mentions a no-hit baseball game, it will cause the pitcher to give up a hit.

Superstitions fall into four categories. Some superstitions focus on important milestones such as birth, death, or marriage. For example: a person born on a Sunday will always be graced with good luck; on the day of a wedding, the groom should not see the bride prior to the ceremony or bad luck will follow them; and following a death, allow the spirit to leave the room by opening all doors and windows. A superstitious person would observe these practices to ensure safety or happiness as one moves from one stage of life to another.

Some superstitions are considered a type of magic. A newborn baby should always be carried upstairs before being carried downstairs to assure that the child rises in the world and has a successful life. A sick person should not be given cut flowers because the flowers will soon wither and die. Instead, give a potted plant which represents life and hope for recovery. Along the same line, when giving money as a gift, it should always be given in a purse or wallet to ensure that the recipient's purses or wallets will never be empty.

Casual superstitions are deliberate actions that ensure good luck, make something good happen, or avoid bad luck. The custom of throwing rice at weddings was initiated to assure that the couple would have many children. Carry a silver dollar or a rabbit's foot to bring good luck. To avoid bad luck, do not start a vacation on Friday, especially on the 13th. Sometimes casual superstitions are used in an attempt to bring bad luck to someone.

Sign superstitions foretell good or bad luck without any effort by the person involved. For example, finding a four-leaf clover, a horseshoe, or a penny will bring good luck. It is bad luck to spill salt or to break a mirror. Rain is coming soon if there is a ring around the moon, and a howling dog is a sign of death. In some cases the effects of signs can be reversed with an action. For example, after one spills salt he/she can cancel the bad luck by throwing a pinch of salt over the left shoulder.

Superstitions provide a way to overcome fears and insecurities. As long as people fear each other and feel uncertain about the future, superstitions will continue to thrive and new ones, reflective of today's lifestyles, will be created.

Skill: Organizing Data

Name _____

Are You Superstitious?

Using what you learned about superstitions, complete the following graphic organizer. Write examples of each type of superstition under the correct heading.

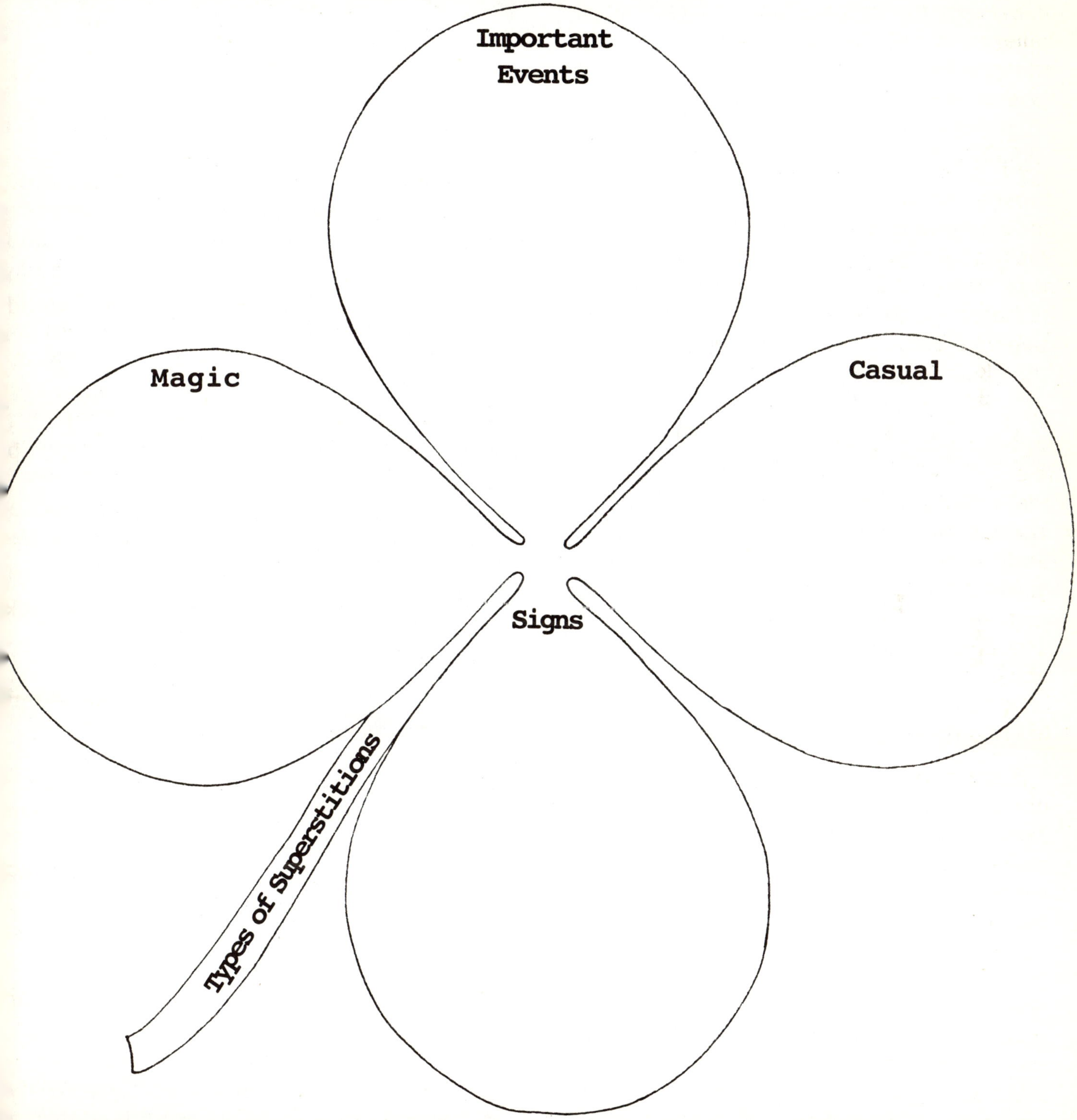

Important Events

Magic

Casual

Signs

Types of Superstitions

Extension: Survey your class and family. Find out what superstitions they practice. Make a chart to present your findings to the class.

Skill: Story Mapping

Name _____

Camping Cousins

Al was the coolest, smoothest dude in all of Minneapolis, Minnesota, and he was my cousin. By the age of 19, Al was a star hockey player on a scholarship at the University of Minnesota and had earned the rank of Eagle Scout. I wanted to be just like him. So when Al asked me to accompany him on a spring fishing trip in northern Minnesota, I was elated!

After planning the trip, we gathered gear and supplies, and embarked on our adventure. We reached the Superior National Forest in northern Minnesota by early evening. We slipped our loaded canoe into the sparkling clear water and paddled straight to our campsite. We set up camp as the sun was setting, and talked about our plans for fishing the next day.

Al, the former Boy Scout, knew all the tricks of an experienced wilderness camper. After we gathered enough wood from the forest floor, he started the campfire using only flint and steel—no matches. For supper we feasted on freeze-dried buffalo, bear stew, beef jerky, hardtack (a hard bread), wild rice, and pea soup. I ate greedily after all that work.

Exhausted, we crawled into our sleeping bags early. Al entertained me with tales of past camping adventures. We were still talking quietly when a sudden north wind picked up, the temperature dropped, and it began to snow. Always alert and innovative, Al found a way to increase the temperature inside the tent. He dragged a log from the woods to the opposite side of the campfire, and laid it across some rocks so it would be off the ground. Then he wrapped aluminum foil around the log. The heat from the fire reflected off the foil and into the tent. The tent became so toasty that I was able to lie on top of my sleeping bag. Soon thoughts of lake trout filled my dreams.

The snow had stopped, but sometime later powerful winds kicked up the flames of our dying fire. I was still engrossed in dreams of a 20-pound fish when I was abruptly awakened by Al. A spark had ignited our tent, and flames had begun engulfing it. Frightened by the flames, I bolted out the tent opening! The tent collapsed with Al inside. Without any thought of endangering myself, I reached into the burning tent, grabbed him, and dragged him to the icy lake. Frightened and bewildered, we checked ourselves and were relieved to find we were not seriously hurt.

Later as we stood by the blazing tent to keep warm, we considered the predicament we were in. We were in the middle of nowhere, with only underwear on our slightly charred, shivering bodies, and all our supplies grilled to ashes. Even Al was unsure of what to do next.

Suddenly, we heard a noise in the forest that sounded like an approaching motor. Anxiously we listened and stared into the darkness intently. Soon we spotted a Jeep traveling down the forest trail. A forest ranger had spied the fire and came to investigate. We quickly jumped into the warm vehicle as the forester drove us to the ranger station where we put on jackets and called our parents.

Al and I had many more camping experiences together, but this one was a turning point for us. It was after this adventure that Al began to treat me more as a friend than a younger cousin, a bond that still holds to this day.

© Instructional Fair, Inc.

Skill: Story Mapping

Name _____

Camping Cousins

Complete the story map.

Characters: 1. _____   Setting: 1. Time: _____

2. _____   2. Place: _____

Events:

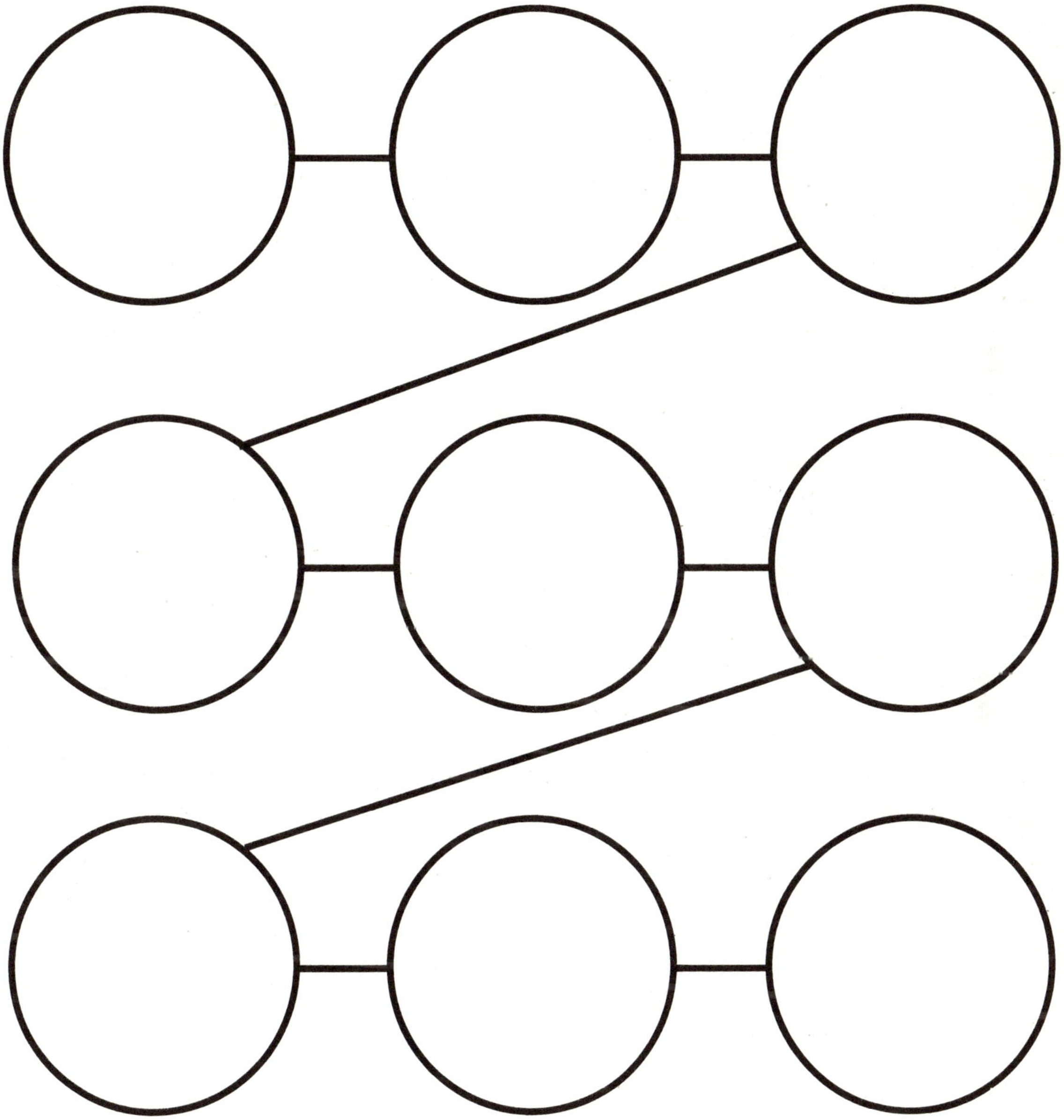

Ending: _____

Extension: Plan a camping demonstration speech. You may choose to demonstrate how to build a fire without matches, set up a tent, pack a backpack or canoe to conserve space, use a compass, and so on. Make an outline, gather your materials, and give your presentation to the class.

Skill: Critical Thinking

Name _____

Cast in Concrete

My family was returning from a vacation in northern Wisconsin when we passed through the small town of Phillips. The town was barely a speck on the highway map. We had already passed through the town when Dad suddenly pulled the car over to the side of the road. We all knew what that meant; he had seen some roadside attraction and we all were going to be subjected to yet another "slice of American pie." Sure enough, he turned the car around.

The sign announced the "eleventh marvel of the world." "Great! Come on kids, let's see what this is all about," encouraged Dad. My two brothers and I, escorted by Dad, stepped out into the 16-acre county park to view three and a half acres of whimsical sculpture. Wisconsin Concrete Park is home to over 200 hand-crafted, concrete statues and creations, all bigger than life. The statues were creatively decorated with old beer bottles and shards of colorful glass. This was truly a marvel.

The welcome sign to the park informed us that this was the creation and the original homestead of Fred Smith, a creative, energetic man who during his life worked as a farmer, lumberjack, musician, tavern owner, and finally sculptor.

We learned that Smith's creations are called "grassroots art." Grassroots artists seldom have any formal art training, but rather, search for their own personal expression of an art form. Much of grassroots art is created by older, retired people and is done for their own satisfaction. Fred Smith sought to create a world of his own, apart from the cultural norms.

He succeeded in creating something new and awe-inspiring. The glass glittered brightly on an eight-horse Budweiser team and wagon. Whole, but empty bottles protruded from the necks of the horses to suggest braided manes. We saw other elegant animals as well: a moose, an elk, and his first piece, a large antlered deer jumping over a log. A statue of lumberjack legend Paul Bunyan stood over twenty feet tall. Hundreds of red, shiny reflectors adorned Bunyan's hunting jacket. Farther into the park, Fred Smith's patriotism was evident in his creations of the Statue of Liberty, an American bald eagle, Abe and Mary Lincoln, and the raising of the flag at Iwo Jima. The afternoon sun played spectacularly over the statuary made with the colored glass.

At the exit gate of the park, there was a sign asking for donations to preserve Fred Smith's surprisingly fragile art. I threw in my loose change. Smith never charged admission and never sold any of his works of art. He established his stone park to meet his need to express himself, and for the enjoyment of others. We did enjoy our impulsive stop at this little "slice of American pie."

Skill: Critical Thinking

Name _____

Cast in Concrete

Define Grassroots art.
_____
_____
_____

Describe Fred Smith's "expression" of art.
_____
_____
_____

What evidence suggests Fred Smith was patriotic?
_____
_____
_____

Explain why the author made this statement:

"... Dad suddenly pulled the car over to the side of the road. We all knew what that meant."
_____
_____

What kinds of work besides sculpting did Fred Smith do during his lifetime?
_____
_____

Why do you think the storyteller threw in a donation?
_____
_____

Extension: Design a grassroots art park for your own yard. Describe what it would look like.

Skill: Changing the Outcome

The South Tower

Name _____

To Jenny, a real vacation meant climbing Mt. Rainier, whitewater rafting, or maybe even going on an African safari. Unfortunately, her parents' idea of a vacation was to visit relatives. So today Jenny, her little brother Adam, and her mom and dad would leave for Ohio to visit Mom's side of the family. Jenny would have to find her own adventure in the bed and breakfast a few blocks from Jenny's aunt and uncle's house.

They arrived in Grandville in the early evening and drove straight to the bed and breakfast. The huge Victorian house was spectacular. A large porch stretched across the front. Tall, round tower rooms rose on either end. As Jenny's eyes traced the elaborate scrollwork, something caught her eye in the south tower window. It must have been the wind blowing the curtain.

Jenny's family had the front half of the top floor to themselves, and Jenny claimed the tower bedroom. She wanted to imagine life as a Victorian woman. A musty odor greeted her as she opened the door and looked around the room. It contained a canopy bed, an antique cradle, and a fireplace on the wall opposite the bed. Chairs positioned around a beautiful rug created a cozy sitting room adjacent to the bedroom.

After a long day in the car with her whining brother, Jenny was ready to go to bed early. Jenny had just settled in her bed when she heard a noise coming from the sitting room. When no one responded to her call, she got up to investigate. Nobody was there, but the adjoining door was open and again she detected that same musty smell. Back in her bedroom, Jenny discovered the cradle rocking gently back and forth. "Must have bumped it," she murmured as she climbed back into bed and turned out the light.

Jenny found the next few days with her relatives uneventful, but the nights in her tower bedroom were different. Minor, unexplainable things happened. The light had been turned off when Jenny knew she had left it on. The comforter had been pulled back after she was positive she had made the bed. The musty smell came and went, and the cradle continued to rock, especially in the middle of the night. Jenny sensed that she was never really alone in the tower room.

On the night before she and her family were to leave for home, Jenny decided to turn in early. While thinking about how she was going to miss this beautiful room, Jenny clearly heard the sound of a crying baby. Suddenly, a thin, translucent form appeared hovering over the cradle right next to her bed. The cradle began to rock and a soothing melody filled the room. Soon, the crying stopped, and the form vanished. Jenny smiled and fell asleep to the sound of the gently rocking cradle.

The next morning as Jenny helped to load the car in preparation for the trip home, she thought about how to tell her parents about the events of the previous night. She finally decided to keep the strange episode to herself. It was her private adventure. Getting into the car, Jenny took one final look at the house. Her eyes were drawn to the south tower window. She saw the curtain move. . .

© Instructional Fair, Inc.

Skill: Changing the Outcome

Name _____

The South Tower

Change the ending of the story. Do this by inventing a new character who enters the story and changes the action.

Write the name and a description of the new character.
_____
_____

Explain where in the story this new character appears.
_____
_____

Describe how the story action will change with the addition of this character.
_____
_____
_____
_____

Rewrite the ending.
_____
_____
_____
_____
_____
_____
_____
_____
_____

Extension: Research a haunted bed and breakfast. Write a description of the happenings reportedly caused by ghosts.

Skill: Vocabulary

Name _____

High-Tech Danger

During my 15th summer the computer changed my life. I had found the Internet. Mom was always prodding me to go outside and get some exercise. Maybe my body wasn't getting any exercise, but my mind was. Hours on the computer seemed like minutes to me. Engrossed by its wealth of information and variety of adventures, I clung to my computer like a baby clings to its mother. Mom thought I was looking pale and thin; had I taken time to eat today?

Early in the summer the problem intensified when Jeremy and I got off at the wrong bus stop in our hometown of New Orleans. While walking the three extra blocks, we spotted a store that delighted our computer-filled brains. The display window featured virtual reality goggles and gloves, joysticks, and a smorgasbord of computer and video games. The store seemed to reel us in like surrendering fish. The proprietor's clothing and inventory were in complete disarray, but her mannerisms were as smooth as silk. Her voice had a chant-like quality and a fragrant aroma encircled us. We experimented with the various computer games, and I bought one titled "Mystic Manipulator." Outside the store, the sunlight seemed to pierce our eyes and skin. We quickly caught the bus home because I was eager to experiment with my new game.

Immediately I became addicted. Day after day, week after week, I remained glued to the computer screen until it had taken total control of my life. Mystic Manipulator kept me awake most of the night. I refused all calls from my friends and barely responded to my parents' pleas to take food and drink.

Finally, Mom took control and came to my rescue! I hadn't bathed in days, my hair was falling out, and I had lost 20 pounds. Believing I was seriously ill, she dragged me to the doctor who in turn performed a variety of tests. I was suffering from malnutrition and sleep deprivation. Mom insisted I stay at the Center for On-Line Addiction. While I was away, Mom packed up my computer and gave it to my friend Jeremy.

When I returned home a few weeks later, I felt relieved that the computer wasn't a temptation any more. I called up all my friends to apologize. But Jeremy hasn't answered my calls and I haven't seen him for weeks—I wonder why.

Skill: Vocabulary

Name _____

High-Tech Danger

Look up the following five words in the dictionary. Write the definition that fits the story context and use it in a new sentence.

smorgasbord

Definition: _____
Sentence: _____

disarray

Definition: _____
Sentence: _____

proprietor

Definition: _____
Sentence: _____

manipulator

Definition: _____
Sentence: _____

deprivation

Definition: _____
Sentence: _____

Extension: A simile is a figure of speech that uses the words "like" or "as" to compare two unlike objects. Find three similes used in the story and explain what each means.

Simile	Meaning

© Instructional Fair, Inc.   IF5100 Reading Comprehension

Skill: Descriptive Language

Name _____

Ghost Story

I wiped my brow. Stuffy steam heat clung to every inch of the room. The water pipes of the old building moaned and groaned. I had been forewarned about the ghost of Ambrose Hall when I was a freshman at this small Midwestern college. Ever since, I was determined to be the one to actually see the ghost. The hall had once been a girls' dormitory, but after years of stories, eerie night noises and unusual happenings, the hall had been converted into classrooms. At dusk, I explored every creak and moan, working my way to the top floor. It was here where I settled in for the night. It was on this floor that the ghost tale was said to have originated.

Legend has it that decades ago a depressed seminarian took his own life on the top floor of Ambrose Hall. He had hanged himself from the light fixture in his dormitory room late one night. Students in neighboring rooms had overheard him reciting prayers earlier in the evening. They later realized he was preparing himself for death, in a ritual commonly called the last rites. The legend tells that he buried himself. The student's body was found buried in the grounds adjoining the campus chapel. His room was sealed off for several years thereafter.

In every class there is at least one student who tells the decades-old tale of the turmoil broiling within the walls of Ambrose Hall. The most common feature of the story is the blood-curdling scream coming from the fourth-floor blackness. One student reported that while returning to campus late one night, he heard an agonizing scream and saw a hulking apparition in the fourth-floor window which quickly disappeared. Another student, sensing that he was being followed, turned around to see a shadowy figure with a skull-like face. The ghost's eyes resembled a fire glowing behind bars. Former residents of Ambrose Hall claim to have heard a male voice saying prayers followed by a painfully agonizing moan. One storyteller reported seeing rivulets of blood seeping from under the door, and then disappearing.

I must be crazy to be sitting in an old building waiting for a ghost. My imagination can't help becoming overly active in this setting. At nearly midnight, I heard what sounded like crying. The cry became a louder wail which grew into a frightening scream. When the shrill scream came to an abrupt end, a shiver of panic raced through my body. A dark, silent, shadowy figure began to take form in front of me. The sounds of religious chanting seemed to penetrate the quiet room and fill my head. The repetitive rhythm of the chant drew my mind into a trance, and my entire being was overtaken by the cadence.

The next thing I remember was awakening in a room brightly lit by the early morning sun. My mind was somewhat foggy. The events of the previous night were temporarily erased from my memory. Now I have a story to tell about the nights in Ambrose Hall for in my left hand, my fingers were tightly clasped around an old, tattered prayer book.

Skill: Descriptive Language

Name _____

Ghost Story

From each paragraph locate the descriptive words or phrases that the author uses to "paint" this as a ghost story. Write the words on the lines by the appropriate paragraph headings.

Paragraph One _____
_____
_____

Paragraph Two _____
_____
_____

Paragraph Three _____
_____
_____

Paragraph Four _____
_____
_____

Paragraph Five _____
_____
_____

The student telling the story stated "I now have a story to tell about the nights in Ambrose Hall." Summarize this student's story in three sentences.

1. _____
2. _____
3. _____

Extension: Write a paragraph describing how you would arrange to see the ghost of Ambrose Hall.

Skill: Organizing Information

Remarkable Rooms

You may find more comfortable surroundings, but it would be hard to find more unique overnight stays than in these four loony lodgings.

The first hotel is the Jules' Undersea Lodge, named after Jules Verne who authored *Twenty Thousand Leagues Under the Sea.* This two-room lodge is anchored to the floor of a lagoon in Key Largo, Florida. Once an underwater mobile research lab, it was converted to a hotel in 1986. Because its entrance can only be reached by diving 30 feet under the water, guests may pack only the necessities that fit in one small, waterproof suitcase. Guests enjoy watching fish swim by the hotel windows. The television plays only videos with a water theme, such as *The Little Mermaid* and *Splash*. The hotel has room service and its own chef. If you choose to order out for pizza, it is delivered in water-tight containers by hotel employees.

If an underwater adventure is not appealing, perhaps staying at the Ariaú Jungle Tower Hotel in Brazil would be more enticing. All of the 138 rooms in this spacious hotel are built on stilts and brush the treetops of the Amazon rainforest. One room tops a 150-foot tree that sits on the banks of the Rio Negro and can be reached only by boat. For fun, guests have the option of swimming in the pool, playing in the game room, or for the brave at heart, searching for alligators or fishing for piranhas. When in your room, you will be entertained by monkeys swinging past your windows. Guests enjoy food of all kinds at this tropical retreat.

For the budget-minded traveler who only wants a place to sleep, a capsule hotel in Tokyo is the place to go. These rooms resemble microwave ovens from the outside. Just large enough for one person, the inside

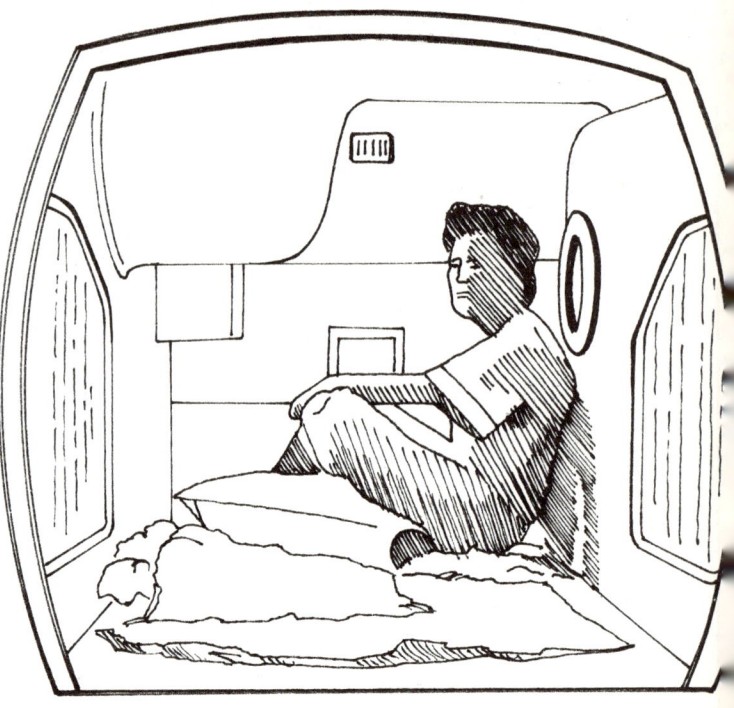

is three feet wide, three feet high and six and a half feet long. These rooms provide an inexpensive night of sleep for Japanese commuters who miss their train home to the suburbs. Each capsule has a small television set and radio. Although room service is not provided, vending machines in the lobby sell snacks.

The Ice Hotel in Jukkasjärvi (you-kas-YER-vee), Sweden, is made entirely from 3,000 tons of ice and snow. None of the rooms is heated. Even the beds in each of the hotel's ten rooms are frozen solid. For warmth, each bed is covered with reindeer skins and sleeping bags. This hotel melts each spring and is totally reconstructed each fall. One year the hotel was about one-fourth the size of a football field. For entertainment, guests may go dog-sledding or on a two-day snowmobiling safari. The hotel's restaurant features several Swedish dishes such as salmon soup and roasted reindeer. Bring warm clothes for this trip!

Skill: Organizing Information

Name _____

Remarkable Rooms

After reading the article about unique hotels, complete the chart below.

Name	Location	Interesting Facts	Activities/Food

Which of these hotels would you choose to stay in? Explain._____
_____
_____
_____

Extension: Design a unique hotel. Draw a picture of your hotel and write an advertisement telling guests about your hotel's location, activities and interesting food.

© Instructional Fair, Inc.   17   IF5100 Reading Comprehension

Skill: Cause and Effect

Name _____

Gold Fever

ROBERT HENDERSON

Something gold was sparkling at the bottom of the miner's pan. After searching all over the world, Robert Henderson finally found gold in northwest Canada, in 1896. One of the first to find gold, he staked his claim at the site, naming it Gold Bottom. Days later when another prospector, George Washington Carmack, struck it rich at nearby Rabbit Creek, history had indeed been made—the gold rush had begun!

News of gold traveled across the United States and Canada, and people from all over caught "gold fever." Leaving their families, thousands of gold-seekers joined what became known as the "great stampede." Visions of quick riches lured the stampeders to the goldfields in the Klondike region of Canada's Yukon Territory.

Freezing temperatures, starvation, and the rugged Chilkoot Pass were enemies of the optimistic prospectors. Because starvation was a major hazard, the Canadian North West Mounted Police ordered that each person should bring along a year's supply of provisions. Some carried as much as 2,500 pounds of food, equipment, and clothing. Without a horse, a prospector would haul about 65 pounds at a time, set it down and go back for the next snow-covered load. He or she would walk thousands of miles back and forth over the Pass. Many discarded items littering the trail were testament to the exhaustion of the men and women.

The prospectors struggled through snow and ice. In 1898, an avalanche buried 70 miners. Ten survived the cascading ice and snow. Other gold-seekers lost noses, fingers, hands or feet to frostbite. Just a brief stop in the freezing wind could be fatal. According to historians, of the 100,000 men and some women who set out seeking gold in the Klondike, only 30,000 to 40,000 actually reached their destination.

Skagway, Alaska was a critical stopping place for gold seekers. Within days of the first gold discovery the town was in chaos. So many thieves, pickpockets, gamblers and swindlers invaded Skagway that it was known as "the roughest place in the world." Other mining towns quickly cropped up in the area. In Dawson, the Klondike's capital, 500 houses were built in six months. When food and supplies became scarce, prices soared sky high. Sled dogs, selling at $350 a piece, soon became unavailable, and miners had to settle for tired old horses.

Reaching the Yukon Territory became easier when the railroad was completed in 1899, but by then the stampede was over. In three short years all the streams had been claimed. For the miner who had struck it rich all the hassles were worthwhile. About $5 million in gold was mined in just two months after the first claims were made, and by 1904, $100 million in gold had been mined from the region. Ten years later all that remained were empty, crumbling buildings and rusty machinery. Today, only a memory is left of the Klondike men and women who risked injury and death in search of that elusive gold metal.

Skill: Cause and Effect

Name _____

Gold Fever

On your copy of the story "Gold Fever," use a highlighter to mark the dates and time periods indicated below. Then, write what happened at that time, and the result.

Time	Action	Result
1896		
within days of the first gold discovery		
two months after the first claims were made		
1898		
1899		
1904		
ten years later		

1. When the prospectors invaded the northwestern region of Canada, what other job opportunities do you think became available? _____
_____
_____

2. On the back of this paper, make a list of provisions that you would need to survive a year in the Yukon Territory.

Extension: Write a letter for more information about the Chilkoot Pass.

Superintendent
Klondike Gold Rush National Historical Park
P.O. Box 517
Skagway, AK   99840-0517 Ph. (907) 983-2921

Area Superintendent
Chilkoot Trail National Historic Sites
Canadian Parks Service
205-300 Main Street
Whitehorse, Yukon Y1A2B5
Ph. (403) 667-3910

© Instructional Fair, Inc.   IF5100 Reading Comprehension

Skill: Critical Thinking

Name _____

Do You Read Me?

Ms. Fuentes' students were exceptionally quiet. Their eyes were focused on the high-tech equipment that was carefully arranged throughout the room. On the walls, student-designed graphics announced this as "Fuentes Control Center." Several clocks on the walls correctly tracked the world's time zones. These eighth graders were about to have an experience that was "out of this world."

Jason called into the ham radio microphone, "Whistle Alpha 5 Uniform Tango Quebec, do you read me? Over." No response. The minutes were ticking away. "This is Kilo Kilo Foxtrot X-Ray, do you read me?" Still no response. The students had only an eleven-minute window to attempt communication with the Columbia space shuttle as it passed 180 miles overhead. They waited anxiously for a reply.

Sporadic crackling sounds from the transmitter preceded a voice, "How are you doing kids?" asked shuttle commander Robert Cabana. Spirited cheers and uproarious clapping immediately rose from Ms. Fuentes' class as contact was made.

Select schools across the nation are participating in instructional experiences such as this. Students have the opportunity to talk directly to astronauts onboard shuttle missions. The program is called Shuttle Amateur Radio Experiment or SAREX and was established to stimulate student interest in science technology and communications. The innovative program was sparked by Owen Garriott who carried a ham radio on board the shuttle Columbia and spoke to ham radio operators all over the world.

The students prepared for their minutes of shuttle conversation with many hours of instruction. They tracked the orbit of the shuttle using computer software. They prepared questions based on space research, and some even ate space food. Some students learned about the shuttle's design, its crew, and the purpose of the mission. The students also learned about many aspects of communication.

If the purpose of SAREX is to stimulate students' interest in space projects, it seems to be successfully reaching its goal. By the sounds of the cheers and the smiles on the faces of students selected to participate in the project, this mission has been completed.

Skill: Critical Thinking

Name _____

Do You Read Me?

1. Write a sentence that tells the main idea of this article.
   _____
   _____

2. For what purpose was the Shuttle Amateur Radio Experiment (SAREX) established?
   _____
   _____

3. List the student activities described in this article.
   _____
   _____
   _____
   _____
   _____

4. Why do you think the astronauts are willing to help students in this way?
   _____
   _____
   _____

5. Create a four-word call name that you might use on the ham radio, similar to the "Kilo Kilo Foxtrot X-Ray" used in this story.

   _____ _____ _____ _____

   Explain why you chose this particular identification. _____
   _____

Extension: Plan with your classmates and contact a ham-radio operator in your community. Invite the operator to demonstrate how the equipment works to your class. Prepare questions to ask your guest.

Skill: Evaluation

Name _____

On the Edge

Biking, hiking, skiing, boating, and surfing are just a few of the sports that are being taken to their limits and beyond. Daredevils, often athletes who have outgrown typical sports challenges, are taking part in dangerous competitions just for the fun and thrill of it. These wild, crazy exploits are known as extreme sports.

Extreme sport competitions include a wide variety of events. Mountain biking is the most popular. Bikers may navigate down steep, winding mountain trails at speeds faster than many people would be able to drive a car down those same trails. A street luger will ride a wheeled sled down a steep hill feet first. Some extreme athletes choose sky surfing, a combination of parachuting and surfing. In addition, extreme skiing, snowboarding, and back-country endurance racing are gaining in popularity.

The extreme athlete may seem crazy when you consider how life-threatening these events are. Big-wave surfers are towed by Jet Skis several miles from the coast. There they catch waves on their surfboards often as high as 25 feet. Mark Foo lost his life during a big-wave surfing competition in California. An extreme skier was killed while conducting a pre-competition route-scouting session. In an extreme race called the Eco-Challenge, several competitors were sent to the hospital. Although no one died, at least six people had life-threatening problems such as dehydration and extentional rhabdomyolysis, a condition in which the body begins to digest its own muscle tissue.

Because of the danger, the World Extreme Skiing championships now screen contestants carefully. Not just anyone can enter; entrants must complete an application form that questions experience and training. For

instance, extreme skiers must have mountaineering experience and avalanche training.

Why would athletes choose to compete in such obviously dangerous sports? They are driven by the thrill. They love the speed and challenge. Some like the power of doing something few others have done before them. Also, as extreme sporting events become more organized, they are becoming more lucrative. Equipment makers want the public to see their products being put to the test by these incredible athletes. When ESPN broadcast the Extreme Games, they easily acquired major sponsorships. The athletes take the money because it's there, but most have other, more personal reasons for getting into these sports.

According to many athletes, participating in a sport may be addictive. But in no other sport does the addiction and love for the competition lead so directly to possible serious injury or death. In order to compete, extreme athletes must practice diligently and develop a healthy respect for their sport.

Skill: Evaluation

Name _____

On the Edge

After reading "On the Edge," list the pros and cons of becoming an extreme athlete.

Pros	Cons

Use the information from your chart to write a persuasive paragraph for one side or the other.

_____
_____
_____
_____
_____
_____
_____
_____
_____
_____

Extension: According to the article, extreme athletes are screened with the help of an application form. Select a sport and design a suitable application form that you feel would help determine if the applicant is qualified to compete.

Skill: Inference

Name _____

Life on a Sub

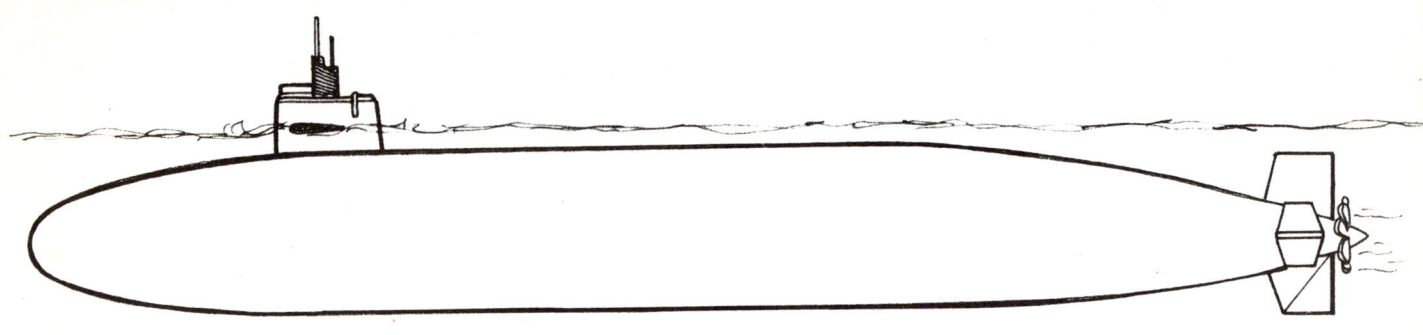

Life on a nuclear submarine can be challenging and exciting. Sailors are trained to handle enemy attacks or spy on installations, but their biggest concern is space! Every inch of space in a submarine is used, twice if possible.

The U.S.S. *Memphis*, a fast attack sub, is 33 feet wide and slightly longer than a football field. Besides the crew of 133, the sub must carry a variety of weapons, computers, navigation and communications gear, and a nuclear reactor. Because it still has to be speedy enough to be called "fast-attack," all the excess weight is "designed out." Some areas of the sub serve "double-duty." The dining room, or crew's mess, also serves as the movie theater. The chairs have oxygen masks stored between their legs. On long voyages, the head, or restroom, also doubles as a storage area for food.

Bedrooms might better be called sleeping capsules. An officer's bedroom, about the size of a walk-in closet, is shared by three people who consider themselves lucky to have so much room. The enlisted men's sleeping quarters are shared by nine sailors. Each curtained bunk is only inches from the sailor in the bunk above; not enough room to roll over! The sailors keep their personal gear in small lockers called puka holes, and their clothes in bunk pans stowed beneath their narrow mattresses. With such close quarters, it is extremely important to be polite.

Being a sub sailor is a unique challenge. In contrast, 3,000 sailors are aboard an aircraft carrier, and each crewman is a specialist. But because there is such a small crew on a submarine, each person is highly trained in a variety of jobs. Many young sailors enjoy submarining because there's always the possibility that even they may be entrusted with steering the $750-million sub.

The purpose of a submarine is two-fold. During a war, a fast-attack sub, using torpedoes, missiles, and mines, is used to attack enemy ships or other subs. In times of peace, submerged subs spy on other ships by listening to ship traffic and monitoring radio transmissions. They also sneak up close to shorelines to spy on military installations.

Because of the stealth required, everyone on board must be quiet. Even the slamming of a door could give away a sub's location in a battle. For that reason, most of the gear is mounted on rubber, and "Think Quiet" signs are found everywhere.

Bubbleheads, as submariners are sometimes called, find that they don't mind a month at a time of cramped living. Potential sub crewmen are tested by psychologists to ensure that they do not have claustrophobia the fear of enclosed places. Giving up space is a small price to pay for the intrigue and chance to run a nuclear submarine.

Skill: Inference

Name _____

Life on a Sub

Pretend that you are a Navy officer in charge of encouraging people to join the Navy and become part of a submarine crew. Using the information from the article, create a dialogue including the advantages you would list trying to convince someone to enlist. Write questions or comments that the potential "bubblehead" might respond with.

Navy Officer	Potential Submarine Sailor

Extension: Design a bedroom for yourself that contains everything you need in as little space as possible. Draw your blueprint neatly and include measurements and dimensions.
- Give dimensions of the room.
- Remember to include the locations of doors and windows.

Skill: Outlining

"Paws With A Cause"

Bending over to pick up an object may seem like a simple task to you but to someone whose mobility is limited, it could mean a loss of balance and a serious fall. That is why some people with disabilities choose to have a well-trained, four-legged companion to act as their hands, legs, eyes, or ears. A dog trained by the Paws With A Cause organization usually has a great impact on the quality of its owner's life.

Paws With A Cause is a non-profit organization that strives to provide specially trained "hearing" and "service" dogs to people with disabilities. The organization began in 1979 in Byron Center, Michigan, and was originally called Ears for the Deaf. The organization initially trained dogs to assist the hearing impaired. Over time, they have expanded their service to training "service" dogs. A service dog enables almost anyone who is physically challenged to gain more independence. In addition, they train combination hearing/service dogs to help individuals with multiple handicaps.

PAWS trainers travel to various animal shelters and humane societies throughout the United States to select dogs. Over 95% of the hearing dogs have been saved from probable death at these shelters. These dogs are then taken to the training center where they spend several months in specific skill training.

The dogs' training consists of three parts. All the dogs are initially given basic obedience training which includes learning to respond to commands such as "sit," "come," and "down." Dogs being trained for the hearing impaired are given specific sound alert training on how to respond to six sounds: door knock, doorbell ring, two types of telephone rings, alarm clock, smoke alarm, and an intruder. The service dogs receive advanced training geared to the individual recipient's needs. They may learn how to turn off lights, retrieve dropped objects, close doors, or serve as a support for walking. Upon the completion of training at the center, the dog and a particular field trainer complete the third phase of training at the recipient's home. The home placement training involves bonding, learning commands, and getting familiar with the needs and routines of the owner.

The cost of purchasing a trained dog is prohibitive to many. A hearing dog costs approximately $5,000, and a service dog is around $8,500. Individuals with disabilities may purchase the dogs with their own money. Paws With A Cause has an active donation fund to assist individuals with the expenses incurred, but the waiting period is quite lengthy. Some organizations will sponsor walk-a-thons or other fund drives to raise money for a member of their community. Also, generous students have earned money through creative methods such as the "Read-a-Million-Minutes" program.

In addition to rescuing many dogs from animal shelters and then training them for specific service, the PAWS organization spends a great deal of time educating the public. Through community awareness presentations, Paws With A Cause is helping the public understand the legal rights of Hearing and Service Dogs and the need for these dogs. With the help of these dogs, having a disability does not mean living with an inability.

Skill: Outlining

Name _____

"Paws With A Cause"

Complete the story map with details from the passage on page 26.

- I. PAWS provides three services:
  - A.
  - B. trains dogs
  - C.
- II. Dogs are trained to serve three types of clients:
  - A.
  - B.
  - C.
- III. Training consists of:
  - A. _____
    1. _____
    2. _____
  - B. _____
    1. _____
    2. _____
  - C. _____
    1. _____
    2. _____

Extension: Write to:
Paws with a Cause Headquarters
1235 100th Street S.E.
Byron Center, MI 49315

- Ask for information on how your school can develop a fundraising campaign.
- Work with a team to organize and carry out your fundraising plan.

Instructional Fair, Inc. 27 IF5100 Reading Comprehension

Skill: Inference

No Ordinary Storm

From his lifeguard station at the shallow end of the pool, Jason noticed clouds gathering in the sky. The community pool had been busy all week because of the muggy, 90-degree weather. Jason was hopeful the temperature might cool off. By the time he took a break at 2:30, the wind was picking up and the sky was darkening. The pool manager announced that the pool was closing immediately due to the severe weather forecast. He wanted everyone safe at home before the storm hit.

All of the swimmers had left by 3:30 except Jason's neighbor, eight-year-old Zack Hill. Zack's mom had dropped him off while she ran several errands. She had planned to pick him up later in the afternoon. The clouds were building fast, and the wind was starting to whip the trees violently. Jason decided to drop Zack off on his way home. They taped a note for Mrs. Hill to the door of the pool office and headed out.

The minute Jason turned out of the parking lot, he suspected this was no ordinary storm. The wind came in strong blasts, the storm clouds were dark and dense, and the sky had turned a bizarre, dark green. The rain hit just as Jason turned onto his block. It came down in sheets, making it difficult to see more than a few inches in front of the car. Worried about the growing fierceness of the storm, Jason decided to keep Zack with him, and he turned into his own drive. He would call Mrs. Hill when she returned to let her know that he would bring Zack home as soon as the storm eased. Jason punched the button of the garage door opener. He impatiently punched it again, but nothing happened. The electricity seemed to be out. They would have to make a run for the front door.

The door was only a few feet away, but the wind was so strong and it was raining so hard that they had to fight their way out of the car and into the house. Jason held Zack's hand firmly. He could feel Zack being tossed by the mighty gusts of wind. The door was heavy with the pressure of the wind. Jason struggled while still grasping Zack's hand. Finally, the door opened, but it was wrenched out of his hands and slammed against the side of the house. The window shattered. With Zack, Jason rushed into the house; his main concern was to get both of them to a safe place.

Jason ran through the house to the basement stairs, pulling Zack after him. With his heart pounding, Jason felt his way down the pitch black stairwell until he found the storage closet under the steps. They were barely inside the cramped space when their ears popped and everything went deadly quiet for a moment. From above, they could hear the sounds of glass breaking and furniture being hurled against the walls. Then a deafening roar, like that of a freight train, blasted through the house. Jason and Zack sat crouched down with their heads tucked under their arms. After the last crash they felt drops of rain on their arms. They looked up and saw a flash of lightening through a crack in the ceiling. The boys braced themselves for what might be next.

It wasn't long before the noise from above seemed to drift away. Jason began to breathe a little easier. He could feel Zack's muscles relax next to him. They made it, and what a story they had to tell!

Skill: Inference

Name _____

No Ordinary Storm

Work with a group of three students to role-play an interview with Jason and Zack. Write at least six questions that a reporter might ask about their experience. Also, write the boys' probable responses based on your interpretation of the reading.

Questions	Responses
1.	1.
2.	2.
3.	3.
4.	4.
5.	5.
6.	6.

Write an ending for "No Ordinary Storm."

_____
_____
_____

Extension: Research tornadoes and hurricanes. Create a Venn diagram to compare the two.

Skill: Reading for Details

Athletes with Attitude

About 43 million Americans have physical or mental disabilities, and millions more suffer from diseases such as diabetes or asthma. But that doesn't seem to prevent some from doing what they want to do, such as playing sports! Many disabled individuals excel in the sports of their choice.

Jim Abbott was born without a right hand. Jim's dream as a child was to play baseball in the major leagues. As a boy, he developed his own system for catching the ball and throwing it back. After catching with his left hand, he would cradle the ball and glove in the crook of his right arm, slip his left hand out of the glove, and immediately grab the ball and throw it. Then Jim would quickly slide his left hand back in the glove so he would be ready to field the ball again. His hours of practice and positive attitude have paid off. He played baseball for the University of Michigan, for the U. S. in the 1987 Pan Am Games, and in the 1988 Summer Olympics. His dream of playing major league baseball was fulfilled in 1989, when he joined the California Angels. Then, as a Yankee pitcher in 1993, he threw a no-hitter against the Cleveland Indians!

Curtis Pride, in his first season as a left fielder for the Montreal Expos, hit a two-run double that helped the Expos beat the Philadelphia Phillies. When given a five-minute ovation by the fans, Curtis could not hear the crowd because he was born 95 percent deaf. His statistics prove that his hearing is not a handicap on the playing field. In 119 minor league games, he stole 50 bases, hit .329, with 21 home runs and 61 RBIs. He believes that anyone can be successful if they put their mind to it.

Tracy MacLeod played basketball with an artificial leg for the women's team at Brandon University, in Manitoba, Canada. Tracy

broke her leg during a basketball game in 1993. After developing circulation problems, doctors operated nine times, but were eventually forced to amputate below the knee. Shocked, angry, but determined, she not only learned to walk on her prosthesis, but to play basketball. Just 8½ weeks after the amputation, she showed up for practice and made her college team. Her motto was, "Just as long as I try." Her superior attitude enabled her to average 4.9 points, 1.9 rebounds, and 12 minutes playing time per game.

Disabled athletes have affected the world of sports for over a hundred years. William Hoy, a deaf baseball player who played in the mid-1880s, asked his third-base coach to use arm signals to tell him what the umpire had called whenever he was at bat. Just ten years later, most umpires were using arm signals for all of their calls. Paul Hubbard, a quarterback in the 1890s for Gallaudet, a college for the deaf, is credited with using the huddle for the first time. He used it to prevent deaf opponents from stealing the hand signals he used to call plays. The huddle was quickly adopted by every team, whether deaf or not.

Famous athletes with disabilities have become heroes and positive role models for many, disabled or not. Some do not consider themselves handicapped because they still accomplish the goals that they set for themselves. Undoubtedly, people who are physically or mentally challenged must work harder than most everyone else. But that doesn't stop them from chasing their dreams and becoming the best that they can be!

Skill: Reading for Details

Name _____

Athletes with Attitude

Complete the chart with information from the article.

Athlete	Disability	Obstacles in Sport	Achievements	Attitude

Write a paragraph about one of your personal goals. Describe the steps and attitude you'll need to reach your goal.

_____
_____
_____
_____
_____
_____
_____

Extension: Write about someone you know who is physically or mentally challenged. Describe the handicap and the challenges encountered daily.

Skill: Critical Thinking

Name _____

Building a Legend

In the final match of the 1994 U.S. Amateur Golf Tournament, 18-year-old Tiger Woods was down six holes. His father leaned over and whispered, "Let the legend grow." Tiger responded to the encouragement and won by two strokes. The greatest comeback in the 99-year history of the tournament was performed by the youngest player ever to win this prestigious golf title. He also made golf history as the first black champion.

Tiger was born Eldrich Woods, in Cypress, California, the only son of Earl and Tida Woods. Tiger is of unusual heritage. His father is part Chinese, Native American, and black American. His mother is part Thai, Chinese, and white American. The nickname Tiger was in honor of his father's South Vietnamese combat partner, Nguyen "Tiger" Phong. After the war, Tiger's father lost contact with his former buddy. He hoped that one day Nguyen would read the name of Tiger Woods in the paper and know he was Earl's son, his namesake.

Tiger Woods was destined to become a legend. He began playing golf at the age of two. At the age of three, he was competing with kids three time his age. He was signing autographs in big block letters at the age of five because he hadn't learned to write cursive yet. By the age of six, Tiger Woods had two holes in one to his credit. By the second grade, he had already won the Junior International golfing title. He became the first boy to win three U.S.G.A. Junior tournaments, pulling them out in the final stages. Tiger Woods appears to be nurturing the idea of becoming the greatest golfer who ever lived.

Tiger has been groomed for golf greatness since the age of nine months. It was his parents' plan to raise the greatest golfer who ever lived. As a youngster he would sit in front of the television and watch videos of the old Master's golf tournaments and practice perfecting his swing in a mirror. He learned to listen to subliminal taped messages about positive psychology with messages like "Expect the best, prepare for the worst." His father drilled him in psychological concentration by attempting to distract him while he golfed. Not only was his game being perfected but also his nerves.

Tiger's training activities have included hours practicing and perfecting his game on the greens, as well as two hours per day of weightlifting, aerobics and stretching exercises. Tiger works daily to build the legend.

Skill: Critical Thinking

Name _____

Building a Legend

A legend generally tells of an exceptional person whose accomplishments are embellished to sound unbelievable. Legends are exaggerations of impressive facts. On this work page, list Tiger Woods' actual accomplishments and his unusual training activities. Then write a colorful legend.

List five golfing accomplishments, activities, or actions.

1. _____
2. _____
3. _____
4. _____
5. _____

List five training activities that have contributed to his golfing skill.

1. _____
2. _____
3. _____
4. _____
5. _____

Take the above attributes and add exaggerations to write your version of the *Legend of Tiger Woods*.

_____
_____
_____
_____
_____
_____

Extension: The sport of golf has its own vocabulary. Research the sport of golf to create a list of golfing terms. Then define each term.

Instructional Fair, Inc.   IF5100 Reading Comprehension

Skill: Comparing

Name _____

A Quirk of Nature

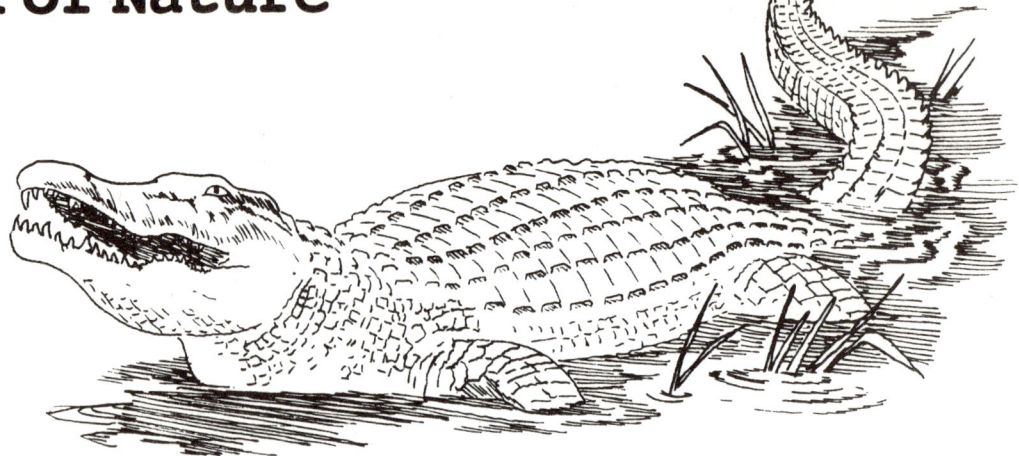

In late August, 1987, three unsuspecting fishermen made an astounding discovery. The men were fishing near Houma, Louisiana, off land owned by the Louisiana Land and Exploration Company when they uncovered a nest that held 18 white alligators and numerous normal-colored brothers. Even more remarkable was the fact that these white alligators had blue eyes.

Audubon Zoo authorities determined that the white alligators were a never before seen genetic mutation of the American alligator. This extremely rare mutation, called leucism is similar to albinism, but even more rare. While albinos have white skin and pinkish-yellow eyes, white leucistic animals have pigmented eyes. And although the nest area has been closely watched since these were found, no additional whites have been seen.

Why have leucistic alligators never been seen before? First of all, this mutation is very rare, so there are few born. Second, mother gators guard babies for awhile, but babies are on their own at a very young age. The 8 to 10-inch white baby alligator is easily spotted by enemies in the dark-colored swamp. Its normal-colored siblings, with their yellow and black stripes blend with their surroundings and gain safety. More whites may have been born, but they probably fell victim to their enemies.

The captive alligators became easier to distinguish from one another over time since as they grew they varied in size and coloration. At six years of age, the smallest of the white alligators measured five feet in length and weighed about 50-60 pounds. The largest was as long as eight feet with a weight of 250 pounds. Each alligator is also distinguished by dark spots and black areas around its head and neck. Everyone who has worked with these unusual creatures agrees that their temperament is very different from that of normal, slow-moving and easy-going alligators. The whites are more feisty and volatile, much like crocodiles.

The general public has become more aware of the existence of these unusual specimens through television appearances and zoo displays. The Louisiana Land and Exploration Company cares for fourteen of the gators at their alligator farm. They donated the other four to the Audubon Institute. Of those four, two are on display at the Audubon Zoo and two can be seen at the Audubon's Aquarium of the Americas. The alligators are also on loan to other zoos and aquariums in the United States and even Japan. People all over the world are able to observe and learn about these remarkable, white mysteries of the swamp.

Skill: Comparing

Name _____

A Quirk of Nature

Write facts in the Venn diagram to compare the leucistic alligators with normal-colored alligators.

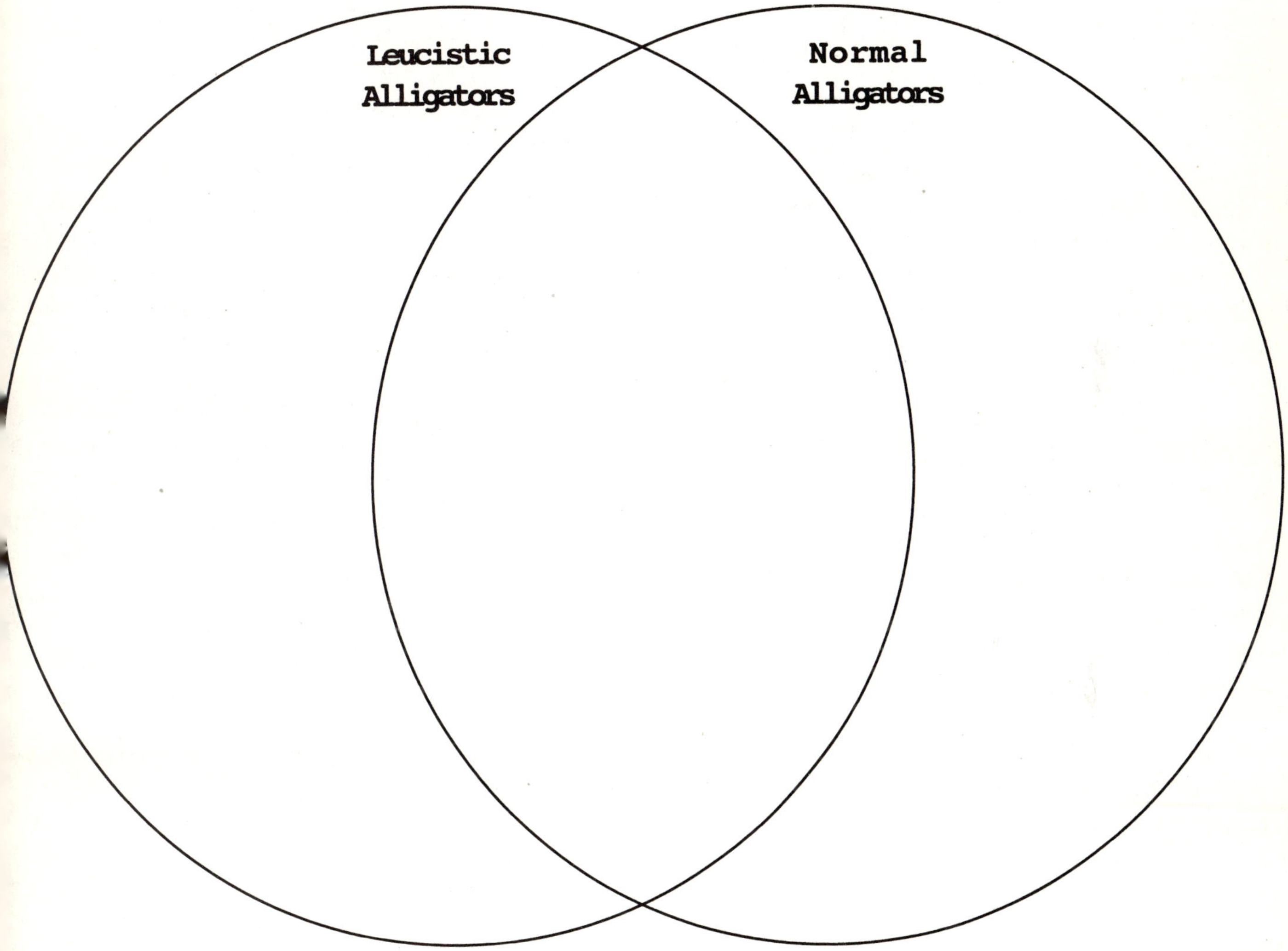

Leucistic Alligators | Normal Alligators

Extension: Learn about other leucistic and albino animals. Possible sources include magazine and newspaper articles, or interviews with veterinarians and zoo officials. Write a report to present to your class.

Skill: Summarizing

Name _____

Underwater Sleuth

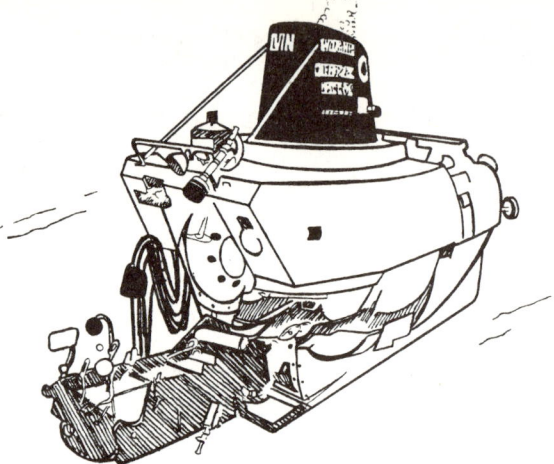

Robert Ballard encounters much danger in his job as detective. He is not the usual kind of detective you are familiar with. He looks for clues in the oceans and seeks scientific adventure with other oceanographers.

Exciting scientific discovery is waiting for the curious on the ocean floor. Ballard was the first to dive to the Mid-Ocean Ridge, the world's longest mountain range which runs 36,000 miles across the floors of the Atlantic, Pacific, and Indian Oceans. In 1977, he made his greatest discovery near the Galapagos Islands. Diving 8,000 feet below the sea, Ballard discovered cracks, or hydrothermal vents, which spewed hot mineral water. In complete darkness, giant worms and clams fed on the minerals. His discovery represented the deepest eco-system ever found.

Ballard specializes in finding and exploring shipwrecks. In 1985, he spent months bouncing sound waves off the Atlantic Ocean floor until he found the famous *Titanic*. A remote-control camera spotted the 46,000-ton wreck that had been buried under water for 73 years. His published photographs of the broken ship made him famous. Also in the Atlantic, he found the *Bismarck,* a German battleship sunk in World War II. He also explored the British luxury liner, the *Lusitania,* sunk by the Germans during World War I. In the Mediterranean, he located the remains of several ancient Roman boats.

But danger lurks beneath these deep bodies of water. On one dive, 9,000 feet down in the Atlantic Ocean, Ballard nearly lost his life when his oxygen mask failed to operate. His crew was probing an underwater mountain when fire spontaneously broke out, filling the craft with smoke. A frantic Ballard cried for help; luckily another scientist was able to turn on Ballard's mask for him. Another time, Ballard crashed his submersible craft into an underwater volcano. He skillfully piloted the damaged craft to the surface, quite shaken by the experience. Because of the dangers, he prefers to send down remote-control robots to explore the deepest waters.

Ballard likes to share his knowledge with others. He began the Jason Project which connects students with live broadcasts of scientific explorations. Students are able to ask questions and operate an underwater probe by remote control. In addition, Ballard acts as a consultant for a weekly television series about a submarine crew in the 21st century. Ballard is pleased that through his accomplishments and programs, he is helping to debunk the notion that scientists and engineers are nerds.

The earth's surface is nearly 75 percent water, yet less than one percent of that area has been explored. Ballard feels that the oceans are the "true frontier" and has proven himself to be a master explorer.

© Instructional Fair, Inc.   IF5100 Reading Comprehension

Skill: Summarizing

Name _____

Underwater Sleuth

Write the main idea of each paragraph from the passage. Then write a summary of the whole article.

1. _____

2. _____

3. _____

4. _____

5. _____

6. _____

Summary: _____

Extension: Look up *oceanographer* in a variety of resources. Write a paragraph that includes a job description, educational requirements, and personal reaction to your findings about work as an oceanographer.

Instructional Fair, Inc.   IF5100 Reading Comprehension

Skill: Reading for Details

Tour of Duty

In August of 1967, Corporal Harry Lewis was dropped into harsh reality after a thirty-day leave to visit his family. His first sight of the Da Nang Air Base in South Vietnam was a group of chained Viet Cong prisoners with black hoods covering their heads. They were closely supervised by U.S. Military Police carrying M-16 automatic rifles. This war-torn country was quite a contrast from his small, peaceful, Iowa town.

The very next day, Harry was transported by plane from Da Nang to his base camp in the Province of Quang Tri. This mountainous region, just south of the North-South division of the country was considered no man's land. However, Harry was not given much of a chance to find out why. Upon his arrival, he learned that his orders had been changed. He was to leave at the end of the week for Dong Ha, which was only seven miles south of the Demilitarized Zone.

Harry did not have time to ask what this move might mean in terms of his safety. He spent the next two days loading equipment and supplies into trucks that would carry the needed materials and men. When he was not working, Harry tried to get some sleep. He was assigned a cot in the transit area, but the deafening noise from the out-going artillery rounds made sleep impossible. The week dragged on endlessly.

Finally, the day came for the convoy to leave the base. For their safety, a mine-sweeper led the long line of military vehicles. Observation helicopters flew overhead, looking for possible ambush sights. The convoy included trucks with .30-caliber machine guns mounted on the roof which further protected the men from enemy attack. Like a funeral procession, Harry's truck which was positioned near the rear of the 75-vehicle line, moved at an agonizingly slow pace.

As they traveled, many Vietnamese people came to the edge of the road to watch the convoy. Women and children, dressed in black clothing and large hats, were begging for food and cigarettes. The begging grew more pronounced as they drove through the small, poverty-stricken villages that dotted the countryside. Several of the American soldiers threw C-rations to the villagers in a small attempt to help.

Several times throughout the day the convoy came to a complete halt. Most of the time Harry did not know the reason for the delay and he felt like a sitting duck, but sometimes word would filter back. One time a large bomb had been located. The military vehicles were forced to drive very slowly and carefully around it. Another time, the convoy stopped for the capture of a Viet Cong who was planting explosives under a bridge in an attempt to isolate and ambush the group. Harry knew if there was one Viet Cong, there would be many more watching and waiting.

At dusk, with everyone's nerves on edge, the convoy finally arrived at Dong Ha. Corporal Harry Lewis sat on a cot with his head in his hands, thinking about the grueling 70 mile trip he had just completed. He wondered what awaited him in the year ahead.

Skill: Reading for Details

Name _____

Tour of Duty

Write journal entries for Corporal Harry Lewis' first five days in Vietnam. Include his activities and probable thoughts.

Day 1
_____
_____
_____
_____

Day 2
_____
_____
_____
_____
_____

Days 3 and 4
_____
_____
_____
_____
_____
_____
_____

Day 5
_____
_____
_____
_____
_____

Extension: Using a resource of your choice, locate Vietnam. Write a descriptive paragraph identifying its relative location.

Instructional Fair, Inc.　　　　39　　　　IF5100 Reading Comprehension

Skill: Semantic Mapping

Name _____

Survival

Before reading this selection, follow the directions on page 41.

What would you do if you were unexpectedly stranded in the wilderness? You have probably read or heard about people who survive under seemingly impossible conditions. Perhaps they have had some survival training. Knowledge of survival techniques is like fire insurance. You may never need it, but if the situation ever arises, you can't get by without it. There are three survival necessities: water, food, and shelter.

Water is one of the few substances necessary to sustain life, but pure water may be difficult to find in some areas. Water should be boiled for three to five minutes before drinking to purify it, if possible. If there is a shortage of water, try not to overexert yourself. Overexertion will cause you to perspire excessively, resulting in a salt deficiency that can cause cramping, fatigue, and dehydration. To control your thirst, drink plenty of water when it is available, rather than sipping over time.

Feelings of hunger can usually be ignored with a positive attitude. Some people might have to overcome their aversion to eating certain animals that are easy to catch. In order to stay alive, survivors must gather "fast" foods so their energy is not being wasted on the "hunt" for food or drink. Insects, such as grasshoppers, wood grubs, ants, bees, and nearly all aquatic insects, are edible. Earthworms, frogs, tadpoles, and minnows can also be eaten. To improve flavor and destroy any possible germs, the critters could be boiled or roasted on a stick, or laid on top of a flat rock set in a fire.

Plants should not be eaten unless they are definitely identified as edible. Nuts, such as acorns, beech, butternut, and hazelnut are easily identified and nutritious. Knobby berries such as blackberries and raspberries are also easy to recognize. More unusual plant parts that are edible are inner tree bark and the fresh shoots of young pine saplings. Inner tree bark is most tender and juicy in the spring, and the pine sapling shoots can be eaten raw, but are better if they are boiled. Any species of pine needles can be simmered in hot water to produce a tea that is rich in vitamin C. Cattails, found in many wild areas, can be used in a variety of ways: the young flower heads and tender stalks can be eaten raw or cooked; the pollen can be used to thicken and add flavor to stews and soups; and the main roots can be peeled, crushed, and cooked, while the smaller, white offshoots can be eaten raw.

When stranded, protection from extreme temperatures may be necessary. In emergency situations involving rain, wind or snow, you can do what the local animals do—crawl under the snow or vegetation in the area. A make-shift cave can be made by tunneling into the base of a thick, evergreen tree and then using tree boughs to line and insulate the cave. When you need protection from the hot sun, a piece of clothing or other fabric can be used as a covering. The center can be propped up by using a pole, then the edges could be anchored by rocks. Later, you can find or build more suitable shelter.

Remaining calm and positive is extremely important in any emergency situation. Assess the severity of your situation calmly, observe your surroundings, and devise a plan. Don't waste time or energy getting upset. When gathering food or building a shelter, use as little time and energy as possible. Employing common sense, and conserving energy may save your life!

Skill: Semantic Mapping

Name _____

Survival

Before reading: Copy the headings from the semantic map below on another piece of paper and write what you already know about these survival necessities.

While reading: Think about the headings.

After reading: While skimming the article use a highlighter to mark the words or phrases that fall under each heading. Then complete this map by writing details under each heading.

Water	Shelter

Survival Necessities

Food

Why are level-headedness and a positive attitude important in any emergency situation?

_____

_____

_____

Extension: Research edible plants. Illustrate and label a page of edible foods found in your area. If possible, collect samples and make an attractive display to teach others.

Skill: Comparing

Name _____

Dinsmoor's Garden of Eden

Travelers through Lucas, Kansas can now visit the Garden of Eden. This is not the paradise described in Genesis. In this beginning there was the 64-year-old creator, S.P. Dinsmoor. Dinsmoor's Garden of Eden is a twist on the Bible's Eden. His tree of life supports an octopus rather than a serpent.

Dinsmoor started building his version of the Garden of Eden in 1907. After laboring twenty-two years to craft his garden, Dinsmoor rested.

Dinsmoor's grassroots art form began when he fashioned his home out of logs made of limestone and concrete. His unusual home resembled a pioneer log cabin. Then he was inspired to plant a garden, not with flowers, shrubs and trees, but rather with a slab of concrete. On his slab yard he sculpted trees out of concrete, which in turn supported concrete and stone birds, flags, angels, and Indians. This unconventional format served to demonstrate his social commentary.

S.P. Dinsmoor was a Populist politician with controversial opinions. In his social commentary, the "Goddess of Liberty" smites the head of an octopus who represents the corporate trusts that controlled early American businesses. Also in the concrete garden, the "Crucifixion of Labor" sculpture represents the working person who Dinsmore believed was victimized by bankers, doctors, lawyers and preachers.

The limestone-concrete mixture has amazingly avoided deterioration over the years. The secret of its longevity is buried with Dinsmore. Is it something in the water? It may be, because his idea spread like concrete dandelions through the small town of Lucas. Other concrete "gardens" have sprung up near S.P. Dinsmoor's unique work of art. A ninety-year-old neighboring woman has used concrete to craft small versions of the Rocky Mountains and the Black Hills in her backyard.

S.P. Dinsmoor's unconventional ideas did not stop with his death. He instructed his family to place his body on display, along with his first wife, in a limestone mausoleum. He designed the concrete coffin with a glass top to enable visitors to view his remains. The creator wished to be be on permanent display, along with his unusual Garden of Eden.

Skill: Comparing

Name _____

Dinsmoor's Garden of Eden

The author compared elements of S.P. Dinsmoor's garden with the Garden of Eden in the Biblical Book of Genesis. Fill in the boxes to identify these comparisons.

Genesis' Garden	S.P. Dinsmoor's Garden

Conclude from the reading selection what types of beliefs a Populist might have held. Write these beliefs below.

_____
_____
_____

Extension: Find out more information on this unusual grassroots artist. Write to:

    Garden of Eden
    2nd and Kansas Avenue
    Lucas, KS 67648

Instructional Fair, Inc.   IF5100 Reading Comprehension

Answer Key
Reading Comprehension
Grade 8

Skill: Identifying Who, What, When, Where, How, Why

Name _____

Silence Is Broken

Write an outline for a newspaper article based on the experience in this story. Use complete sentences.

Who: Gary and his five mapping companions

What: found a Russian spy satellite

When: in the winter

Where: northern Canada; 500 miles west of the Hudson Bay and 200 miles from any town.

How: they arrived by canoe and sled dog team

Why: Gary and his companions were mapping and seeking solitude.

Write a headline for your article.
Accept reasonable responses.

Extension: On a map of Canada, locate where Gary's story takes place. Use the clues provided in this story.

Page 3

Skill: Organizing Data

Name _____

Are You Superstitious?

Using what you learned about superstitions, complete the following graphic organizer. Write examples of each type of superstition under the correct heading.

Important Events
- A person born on a Sunday will have good luck.
- Groom should not see bride prior to ceremony
- Open windows after a death

Magic
- A newborn baby is carried upstairs to assure that the child will rise in life.
- Give potted plants to help friends recover
- Give money in a purse to ensure a full purse.

Casual
- Throw rice at weddings
- Rabbit's foot and silver dollar bring luck.
- Avoid starting a vacation on Friday the 13th.

Signs
- Four leaf clover, horseshoe, and penny bring good luck.
- Spilling salt and breaking a mirror bring bad luck.
- Ring around the moon means rain
- Howling dog — death

Types of Superstitions

Extension: Survey your class and family. Find out what superstitions they practice. Make a chart to present your findings to the class.

Page 5

Skill: Story Mapping

Name _____

Camping Cousins

Complete the story map.

Characters: 1. Al
2. younger cousin

Setting: 1. Time: spring
2. Place: northern Minn.

Events:
- Al asked his cousin to come along on a fishing trip
- They planned the trip and left.
- They paddled to the campsite.
- They ate and went to bed.
- Al told camping adventure stories.
- A wind picked up and Al warmed the tent
- The tent caught on fire
- The cousin saved Al from the fire.
- A forest ranger found them.

Answers may vary.

Ending: They developed a friendship based on respect for each other.

Extension: Plan a camping demonstration speech. You may choose to demonstrate how to build a fire without matches, set up a tent, pack a backpack or canoe to conserve space, use a compass, and so on. Make an outline, gather your materials, and give your presentation to the class.

Page 7

Cast in Concrete

Define Grassroots art.
Grassroots art is usually created by an older, retired person with no training who wants to express him/herself.

Describe Fred Smith's "expression" of art.
He crafted over 200 concrete statues embedded with colorful glass and old bottles.

What evidence suggests Fred Smith was patriotic?
He created a Statue of Liberty, an American bald eagle, and Abe and Mary Lincoln and more.

Explain why the author made this statement:
"...Dad suddenly pulled the car over to the side of the road. We all knew what that meant."
Their father must stop frequently at roadside attractions.

What kinds of work besides sculpting did Fred Smith do during his lifetime?
farmer, lumberjack, musician, tavern owner

Why do you think the storyteller threw in a donation?
She liked the sculptures and wanted to support it since Smith never charged admission.

Extension: Design a grassroots art park for your own yard. Describe what it would look like.

Page 9

The South Tower

Change the ending of the story. Do this by inventing a new character who enters the story and changes the action.

Write the name and a description of the new character.
Answers will vary.

Explain where in the story this new character appears.
Answers will vary.

Describe how the story action will change with the addition of this character.
Answers will vary.

Rewrite the ending.
Answers will vary.

Extension: Research a haunted bed and breakfast. Write a description of the happenings reportedly caused by ghosts.

Page 11

High-Tech Danger

Look up the following five words in the dictionary. Write the definition that fits the story context and use it in a new sentence.

smorgasbord
Definition: A varied collection
Sentence: Answers will vary.

disarray
Definition: A state of disorder; confusion
Sentence: Answers will vary.

proprietor
Definition: One who owns and manages a business
Sentence: Answers will vary.

manipulator
Definition: One who controls by a skilled use of hands
Sentence: Answers will vary.

deprivation
Definition: The condition of being deprived, at a loss of
Sentence: Answers will vary.

Extension: A simile is a figure of speech that uses the words "like" or "as" to compare two unlike objects. Find three similes used in the story and explain what each means.

Simile	Meaning
I clung to my computer like a baby to its mother.	She/he never wanted to leave the computer.
The store reeled us in like surrendering fish.	We knew we had no power; it was useless to fight it.
mannerisms were smooth as silk.	She moved smoothly and gracefully.

Page 13

A Ghost Story

From each paragraph locate the descriptive words or phrases that the author uses to "paint" this as a ghost story. Write the words on the lines by the appropriate paragraph headings.

Paragraph One — stuffy steam heat, pipes moaned and groaned, eerie night noises, creak + moan

Paragraph Two — late one night, preparing for death, buried himself

Paragraph Three — decades-old tale, hulking apparition, turmoil broiling, blood-curdling screams, agonizing scream...

Paragraph Four — nearly midnight, wail, frightening scream, shiver of panic, shadowy figure...

Paragraph Five — mind was foggy, nights in Ambrose Hall, tightly clasped, old, tattered book

The student telling the story stated "I now have a story to tell about the nights in Ambrose Hall." Summarize this student's story in three sentences. Answers may vary.

1. The student set out to see the ghost.
2. He spent the night listening and looking.
3. He woke up with the prayer book in hand.

Extension: Write a paragraph describing how you would arrange to see the ghost of Ambrose Hall.

Page 15

Remarkable Rooms

Skill: Organizing Information

After reading the article about unique hotels, complete the chart below.

Name	Location	Interesting Facts	Activities/Food
Jules' Undersea Lodge	on the floor of a lagoon in Key Largo, Florida	• entrance 30 ft. under water • once a mobile research lab • limited to one small suitcase	• watch fish • videos are water-related • Room service and Chef with optional take out
Ariaú Jungle Tower Hotel	Amazon Rainforest, Brazil	• 138 rooms on stilts • one room is 150 feet off the ground	• swim in pool • game room • search for alligators • monkeys • variety of food
Capsule hotel	Tokyo, Japan	• 3' x 3' x 6' • inexpensive • for commuters	• television • radio • vending machines
The Ice Hotel	Jukkasjärvi, Sweden	• Made of 3,000 tons of snow and ice • melts every year • reindeer blankets	• dog sledding • snowmobile • salmon soup • roasted reindeer

Which of these hotels would you choose to stay in? Explain. _Answers will vary._

Extension: Design a unique hotel. Draw a picture of your hotel and write an advertisement telling guests about your hotel's location, activities and interesting food.

Page 17

Gold Fever

Skill: Cause and Effect

On your copy of the story "Gold Fever," use a highlighter to mark the dates and time periods indicated below. Then, write what happened at that time, and the result.

Time	Action	Result
1896	Robert Henderson staked his claim.	The gold rush began.
within days of the first gold discovery	People followed Henderson to gold.	The nearby towns were in chaos.
two months after the first claims were made	$5 million in gold was mined.	More people came.
1898	An avalanche on the pass killed 70.	10 survived. Only 30-40% reached the Klondike
1899	The railroad was completed.	miners could reach the gold territory fast
1904	$100 million in gold mined.	streams were becoming depleted.
ten years later	The area was abandoned and ruined.	The stampede was over.

1. When the prospectors invaded the northwestern region of Canada, what other job opportunities do you think became available? _Answers will vary._ _home sales, stores, clothing, animal caretakers, Drs. etc._

2. On the back of this paper, make a list of provisions that you would need to survive a year in the Yukon Territory. _Answers will vary._

Extension: Write a letter for more information about the Chilkoot Pass.

Superintendent
Klondike Gold Rush National Historical Park
P.O. Box 517
Skagway, AK 99840-0517 Ph. (907) 983-2921

Area Superintendent
Chilkoot Trail National Historic Sites
Canadian Parks Service
205-300 Main Street
Whitehorse, Yukon Y1A2B5
Ph. (403) 667-3910

Page 19

Do You Read Me?

Skill: Critical Thinking

1. Write a sentence that tells the main idea of this article. _Answers may vary._ _Students have the opportunity to communicate with the shuttle crew and learn more about science technology and communications._

2. For what purpose was the Shuttle Amateur Radio Experiment (SAREX) established? _SAREX was established to stimulate student interest in science technology and communications._

3. List the student activities described in this article. _They tracked the orbit of the shuttle. They prepared questions based on research. They ate space food. They learned about the shuttle's design, crew, and purpose. They also learned about communication._

4. Why do you think the astronauts are willing to help students in this way? _Answers will vary._

5. Create a four-word call name that you might use on the ham radio, similar to the "Kilo Kilo Foxtrot X-Ray" used in this story. _Accept reasonable responses._
Explain why you chose this particular identification.

Extension: Plan with your classmates and contact a ham-radio operator in your community. Invite the operator to demonstrate how the equipment works to your class. Prepare questions to ask your guest.

Page 21

On the Edge

Skill: Evaluation

After reading "On the Edge," list the pros and cons of becoming an extreme athlete.

Pros	Cons
• fun, thrilling	• very dangerous
• variety of events	• can lead to death or serious injury to competitors
• contestants are screened	• training can be just as dangerous as competition
• unique events	
• becoming more lucrative	
• travel to various locations.	• must prove oneself before entering competition
• become recognized for ability	• experience may be difficult to acquire
Answers may vary.	

Use the information from your chart to write a persuasive paragraph for one side or the other. _Accept reasonable responses._

Extension: According to the article, extreme athletes are screened with the help of an application form. Select a sport and design a suitable application form that you feel would help determine if the applicant is qualified to compete.

Page 23

© Instructional Fair, Inc.   46   IF5100 Reading Comprehension

Skill: Inference

Life on a Sub

Pretend that you are a Navy officer in charge of encouraging people to join the Navy and become part of a submarine crew. Using the information from the article, create a dialogue including the advantages you would list trying to convince someone to enlist. Write questions or comments that the potential "bubblehead" might respond with.

Navy Officer	Potential Submarine Sailor
Accept reasonable answers.	

Extension: Design a bedroom for yourself that contains everything you need in as little space as possible. Draw your blueprint neatly and include measurements and dimensions.
- Give dimensions of the room.
- Remember to include the locations of doors and windows.

Page 25

Skill: Outlining

"Paws With A Cause"

Complete the story map with details from the passage on page 26.

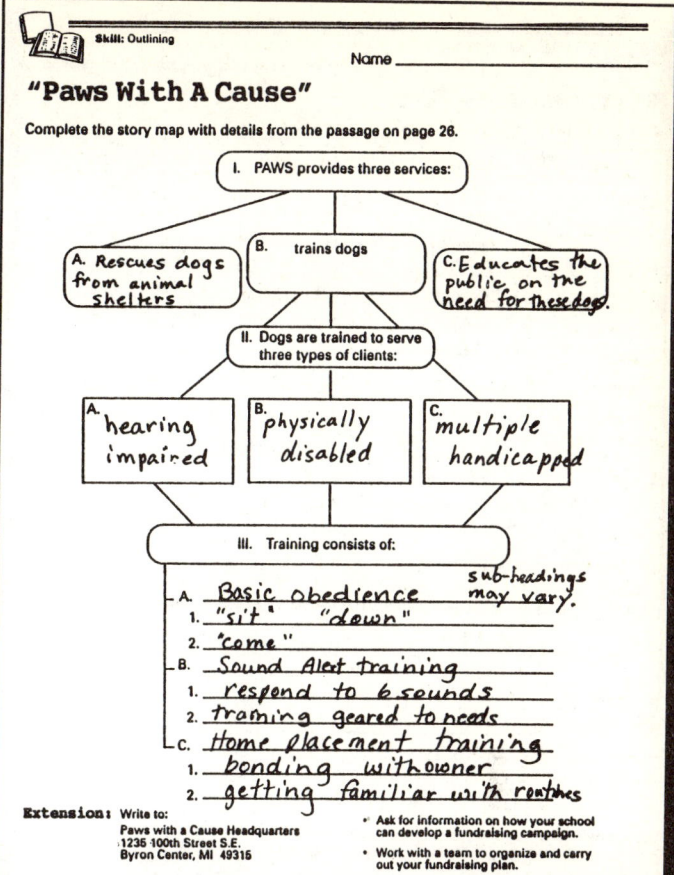

I. PAWS provides three services:
 A. Rescues dogs from animal shelters
 B. trains dogs
 C. Educates the public on the need for these dogs

II. Dogs are trained to serve three types of clients:
 A. hearing impaired
 B. physically disabled
 C. multiple handicapped

III. Training consists of: (sub-headings may vary)
 A. Basic obedience
  1. "sit" "down"
  2. "come"
 B. Sound Alert training
  1. respond to 6 sounds
  2. training geared to needs
 C. Home placement training
  1. bonding with owner
  2. getting familiar with routines

Extension: Write to: Paws with a Cause Headquarters, 1235 100th Street S.E., Byron Center, MI 49315
- Ask for information on how your school can develop a fundraising campaign.
- Work with a team to organize and carry out your fundraising plan.

Page 27

Skill: Inference

No Ordinary Storm

Work with a group of three students to role-play an interview with Jason and Zack. Write at least six questions that a reporter might ask about their experience. Also, write the boys' probable responses based on your interpretation of the reading.

Questions
1. Accept reasonable answers
2.
3.
4.
5.
6.

Responses
1.
2.
3.
4.
5.
6.

Write an ending for "No Ordinary Storm."
Answers will vary.

Extension: Research tornadoes and hurricanes. Create a Venn diagram to compare the two.

Page 29

Skill: Reading for Details

Athletes with Attitude

Complete the chart with information from the article.

Athlete	Disability	Obstacles in Sport	Achievements	Attitude
Jim Abbott	born with no right hand	needed to learn to catch and throw with one hand.	major league Olympics no-hitter	positive attitude, determined
Curtis Pride	95% deaf	can't hear fans, ball + bat, or calls	Stole 50 bases hit .329 21 home runs 61 RBIs	Anyone can be successful if they put their mind to it
Tracy MacLeod	amputated leg below the knee	had to learn to run + jump on a prosthesis	She made her college team.	"Just as long as I try..."
William Hoy	deaf	Couldn't hear ump calls	Now umps use arm signals.	NA
Paul Hubbard	deaf	deaf opponents stole hand signals	He developed the huddle.	NA

Write a paragraph about one of your personal goals. Describe the steps and attitude you'll need to reach your goal.
Accept reasonable responses.

Extension: Write about someone you know who is physically or mentally challenged. Describe the handicap and the challenges encountered daily.

Page 31

Instructional Fair, Inc.   IF5100 Reading Comprehension

Building A Legend

Skill: Critical Thinking

A legend generally tells of an exceptional person whose accomplishments are embellished to sound unbelievable. Legends are exaggerations of impressive facts. On this work page, list Tiger Woods' actual accomplishments and his unusual training activities. Then write a colorful legend.

List five golfing accomplishments, activities, or actions.
1. first male to win three USGA Junior tourn.
2. first black to win the U.S. Amateur Golf tourn.
3. Youngest player to win U.S. Amateur G.T.
4. At 6 he had 2 holes in one
5. By 2nd grade he had won the Jr. International golfing title.

List five training activities that have contributed to his golfing skill.
1. drilled in psychological concentration
2. positive subliminal recordings
3. watched videos of Master's tourn.
4. Physical training 2 hours/day
5. practices golf daily

Take the above attributes and add exaggerations to write your version of the *Legend of Tiger Woods*.

Legends will vary.

Extension: The sport of golf has its own vocabulary. Research the sport of golf to create a list of golfing terms. Then define each term.

Page 33

A Quirk of Nature

Skill: Comparison

Write facts in the Venn diagram to compare the leucistic alligators with normal-colored alligators.

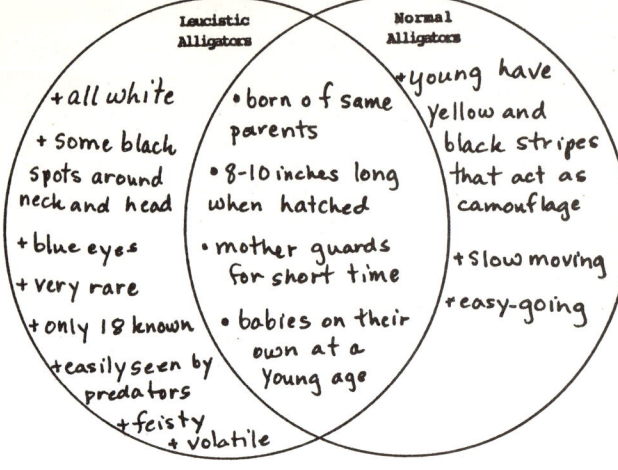

Leucistic Alligators:
+ all white
+ some black spots around neck and head
+ blue eyes
+ very rare
+ only 18 known
+ easily seen by predators
+ feisty
+ volatile

Both:
• born of same parents
• 8-10 inches long when hatched
• mother guards for short time
• babies on their own at a young age

Normal Alligators:
+ young have yellow and black stripes that act as camouflage
+ slow moving
+ easy-going

Extension: Learn about other leucistic and albino animals. Possible sources include magazine and newspaper articles, or interviews with veterinarians and zoo officials. Write a report to present to your class.

Page 35

Underwater Sleuth

Skill: Summarizing

Write the main idea of each paragraph from the passage. Then write a summary of the whole article.

1. Robert Ballard is an underwater detective.
2. There are many exciting things to be discovered under the water.
3. Ballard has found many famous shipwrecks.
4. Oceanographers face many dangers in their explorations.
5. Ballard shares his knowledge through multi-media.
6. There is still much to explore under the oceans' surface.

Summary: Accept reasonable answers.

Extension: Look up *oceanographer* in a variety of resources. Write a paragraph that includes a job description, educational requirements, and personal reaction to your findings about work as an oceanographer.

Page 37

Tour of Duty

Skill: Reading for Details

Write journal entries for Corporal Harry Lewis' first five days in Vietnam. Include his activities and probable thoughts.

Day 1
He arrived at DaNang air base in South Vietnam. He saw a worn-torn country in contrast to his home in Iowa. Answers will vary.

Day 2
Transferred to his base camp which was considered no man's land. His orders were changed. He must prepare to go to Dong Ha. A.W.V.

Days 3 and 4
He is very busy - no time to think or worry about safety. He must load equipment and supplies in trucks. He couldn't sleep because of the noise. Answers will vary.

Day 5
The convoy moved at an agonizingly slow pace with many dangers surrounding them: bombs and enemies. They took all day - 70 miles.

Extension: Using a resource of your choice, locate Vietnam. Write a descriptive paragraph identifying its relative location.

Page 39